The Intellectual Toolkit of Geniuses

40 Principles that Will Make You Smarter and Teach You to Think Like a Genius

By I. C. Robledo

www.Amazon.com/author/icrobledo

The Intellectual Toolkit of Geniuses: 40 Principles that Will Make You Smarter and Teach You to Think Like a Genius

Disclaimer

Table of Contents

An Introduction to the Intellectual Toolkit of Geniuses

If you've ever wanted to learn to think more like a genius, you've come to the right place. Truly smart people have a different way of viewing the world. They ask unique questions. They don't accept simple yes or no answers to tough questions. They always want to learn more, to better themselves, and to prepare themselves for the next great challenge.

Geniuses do not look to take the easy path. They enjoy seeking intellectual challenges. They enjoy finding people that have other points of views, and discovering why they think that way. Geniuses do not assume they have all the answers, or that they are the smartest person. They believe there is always room to grow, to become better and smarter.

A genius is someone who puts in the work. They choose their path and they focus on it with the intensity of a laser beam. The greatest geniuses are those who transform our understanding of reality through experiments, inventions, or discoveries. Some of these would be Charles Darwin, Thomas Edison, Albert Einstein, and William Shakespeare. Realize that genius can be learned. The greatest geniuses use principles to guide their thinking, and in this book you will learn them.

I came up with these principles from researching geniuses in history, interacting with geniuses, and studying geniuses. They have shared with me their collective intellectual toolkit, and now I want to share it with you so you can become one step closer to genius.

Principle #1: Don't make assumptions.

To see things as they are, avoid assuming that you know what someone is thinking, or that you know their motivations. You may have clues or ideas, but you should avoid making assumptions until you have enough information to be sure you know what is really happening. Assumptions will make you feel like a fool when you are wrong. They will also be a waste of precious brain power, as you will often analyze something that is based on a faulty assumption. If you do that, you will waste more time and resources. Focus your attention elsewhere and you will be more productive. If something is important, be direct and find out what you need to know, rather than assuming.

Principle #2: Learn from multiple formats or methods.

It is true that people learn in different ways. Some learn better through reading, others through listening, seeing, or doing. When learning something new, it is a good idea to start with one method of learning, perhaps your favorite first. When you come across a barrier where you don't understand, try another way. Keep doing this until you make progress and finally understand. Even just with the internet you can use books, Wikipedia, YouTube, and free Open Courseware. You will learn more quickly and holistically through multiple sources. Understand that the real world will not allow you to choose how to learn from it. At work you may be asked to attend conferences or to read some material. Either way, you will be expected to learn even if it isn't your preferred way.

Principle #3: Learn to be self-reliant and to prioritize what is most important.

School, work, government, and other systems have their own agendas, and their own flaws. They will be happy to tell you where to go and what to learn, but at some point you have to decide for yourself what is truly important to know.

School focuses on learning math, science, and history, among other topics, but what about learning *why* those topics are important? They often don't focus on the why, as much as they ask you to simply memorize facts. Survival skills are rarely taught in school, but this is another example of something that could be quite useful to learn. The point here is you need to decide for yourself what is important. Ask what you would teach if you were in charge of the school system. There is no excuse to be passive and let your education slip past you. Take those important topics and learn them for yourself.

Be aware that often times in modern society, trivial things are talked about on and on as if they are important, and truly important things like world issues are rarely discussed in any deep way. Intelligent people tend to strive to find something meaningful and important to them, and they will focus on this instead of trivial issues.

Thomas Edison is a good example of how self-reliant someone can become. He came from a poor family and he didn't have teachers to show him what to learn. He read all kinds of books to satisfy his curiosity about how machines worked. Edison taught himself through his own deep determination to learn. Great geniuses do not make excuses. They are prepared to put in the work and learn on their own if required.

Principle #4: No one weighs the importance of facts for you. Weigh them yourself.

In school you are usually given all the information for a test, and it is up to you to learn it. Tests are often multiple choice, meaning every question is worth just the same as the other. In real life, this isn't how things work. In real life you often have access to information, but you are rarely told what is the most important to know. However, when you are tested in life (given a sort of grade, if you will) the people who do best are the ones who understand what is most important. Also, realize that this is a skill that is never taught anywhere. Learn to weigh the facts for yourself. Observe patterns of what tends to be critical in your work space, or in your household, or in any system. Focus on making sure the most important things are taken care of first.

Principle #5: Read source literature and books.

There is nothing wrong with reading new books. This is a new book, and I read newer material all the time. However, you can often get a better quality learning experience when you go back to older classical reads like *The Odyssey*, anything by Shakespeare, *The Wealth of Nations*, Darwin's *On the Origin of Species*, and Ancient Greco-Roman mythology. Going back gives you a more direct view into some of the greatest minds that came up with original works of great art and science. When you read older works, you also see interesting patterns. You start to see that a lot of classical works are referenced all over the place in modern society. If you aren't aware of them, however, it's easy to miss.

Before You Continue . . .

As a thank you for reading, I want you to have a free guide called:

Step Up Your Learning: Free Tools to Learn Almost Anything

Have you ever wondered what the best sites and resources for learning are? It takes time and effort to figure out which sites are worth it and which are not. I hope to save you some of that time so you can spend more of it learning instead of searching the Internet.

In the past ten years or so, there has been a free learning revolution happening. More and more resources for learning are becoming available to the public at no cost. With so many new ones coming out, it's easy to miss out on some of the great learning opportunities available. Fortunately for you, this guide is short at around 4,000 words, and tells you exactly what you need to know.

The guide stems from my own experiences of using a variety of learning sites and resources. In it, you will discover the best places to go for learning at no cost. Also, I'll explain which resources are best for you, depending on your learning goals.

You can download this free guide as a PDF by typing this website into your browser: http://bit.ly/Robledo

Now, let's get back on topic.

Principle #6: Everyone is constantly trying to sell you something.

We live in a capitalistic society where ads are pretty much everywhere. They are on buses, buildings, on TV, in our computers, etc. Some people literally have ads tattooed on to their bodies. Also, commercial businesses surround us everywhere we go. You probably can't walk a mile in any direction without finding a place that is selling something. A competitive marketplace has forced advertisers to look for more and more creative ways to sell their products. Experienced marketers have learned to appeal to us both consciously and subconsciously, increasing their power over us. We have to learn to resist their influence and to choose our own direction.

You've probably heard that supermarkets strategically place items in the store so the ones everyone always needs like milk are often way in the back. Selling is everywhere, whether you notice it or not. Even if someone isn't trying to sell you a product, they may be trying to sell you an idea. For example, they may try to convince you of their religion, their politics, their world views, etc. We have to be aware of all this selling, so we are not so naïve as to believe that everyone wants to personally help us. Much of the time rather than help, others are focused on selling a product or idea to us.

Principle #7: Intelligence and learning habits can always be improved.

Intelligence and IQ are very misunderstood concepts. Intelligence is a complex human attribute that can't be perfectly defined or perfectly measured. The problem with IQ is that it appears to be an authoritative measurement by psychologists. However, IQ is far from authoritative. It is really just one way to view intelligence. IQ is not a terrible measurement of intelligence, it is just not fully accurate. By presenting the intelligence of a person as one number, we run the risk of limiting our potential. A single number also implies permanence, leading to false views of intelligence. It used to be believed that intelligence was mostly genetic, but this is not the case. Intelligence can be improved, depending on how you choose to use your brain.

The newer research emphasizes the plasticity of the brain. This means that the brain itself is a modifiable structure. The more you use it and challenge it, the more you can build on your intellect. If you give up and you believe you have a limited intelligence, then you won't improve it.

Stephen Hawking is commonly regarded as a genius for his work in physics and black holes. He was once asked what his IQ was. His reply was: "I have no idea. People who boast about their IQ are losers." He clearly doesn't put too much significance on the number. He doesn't even know his own IQ. But the real takeaway message is that when you are a true genius and have true accomplishments, IQ becomes revealed for what it is. That is, just another number.

Principle #8: The knowledge you acquire on your own is the most valuable

Geniuses don't wait around for information to fall on their laps. They also don't rely on one source to tell them everything. For example, they will not just listen to one news station and wait for the information to come to them through that one channel. A genius will pursue all kinds of ways of finding knowledge. They will ask questions and do research to find answers. When they find a direct answer to the question given by an expert, they will not necessarily believe the response without further evidence. They will seek more and more information to see if they truly understand what they think they understand. The knowledge that you seek out and work to find and learn is the most useful and helpful of all. If it comes to you in a pamphlet or through a media station and finds you, then you are more likely to take it in passively and not make much use of it. Also of course, information that finds you is more likely to be biased. The best you can do is seek out the answers to your own questions.

Principle #9: Read a wide range of material, and learn broadly.

Even if your goal is to be an expert in one field, the world is becoming increasingly multidisciplinary. The people that make the greatest breakthrough discoveries often have some understanding of other fields. Einstein was a fantastic violinist in addition to being a leading physicist, for example. Often, what holds back some of the world's experts is that they become so fixated on a narrow subarea within their field, and they don't learn and grow in other areas.

This can be a mistake, because the world is naturally all interrelated. Biology and physics are related. Physics and math are related. Math and music are related. And music and sculpture are related. You get the idea. You can even make the jump that biology and sculpture are interrelated, as da Vinci did, one of the greatest artists, inventors, engineers, and polymaths of all time. He used his understanding of human anatomy to make his paintings and sculptures more vivid and real, and this is what captured people's imaginations when they saw his work. Imagine if he hadn't learned broadly. He may have never become the great artist that we've all heard of.

Principle #10: Be aware of where your advice is coming from.

It is human nature to want to give advice and help others. It makes us feel important and good, much of the time. We have to be careful who we take advice from, as not all advice is good. In general, you can figure that if the advice is too general then it isn't really all that useful anyway. If you receive advice that is very specific, or very radical in some way, you should be careful in how you proceed. That kind of advice should only be considered from an expert, or someone with tremendous experience in an area. If there is a possibility for negative consequences, be even more careful with the advice. Advice that is fairly mild probably doesn't make much of a difference. You've probably heard it before anyway. Be kind, be helpful, eat well, etc.

Always keep in mind where the advice is coming from. The people you can trust the most are those with great experience and great success. Often times, these people are too busy to give much advice, and you have to learn from their actions rather than their words. Either way, remember that every situation is different. Think it through for yourself and decide if any advice is worth pursuing. If it is, it is your choice entirely. The person who gave you the advice cannot be expected to help with any negative outcomes that arise from your taking the advice.

Principle #11: Engage in personal experiments with the world around you.

Do not rely fully on the experiments of scientists, or the word of the media. Science although very valuable to society, is not perfect. Science is run by scientists with their own biases and expectations, and their own careers to run. They are biased to finding what they want to find just as much as you're biased to want to succeed in your own life. In the long run science takes us in the right direction, but the most recent findings should be taken in somewhat skeptically. Rather than rely fully on the new findings of scientists and the media, who use populations that may not even represent you (often rats or college students), you can run your own experiments. It is as simple as trial and error. Try something and see if it works. Start small, don't risk too much on your personal experiments.

The world is constantly changing and evolving, and everyone is in such a unique circumstance, that you may be better off testing for yourself what works and what doesn't, rather than reading what worked for other people who could be completely different from you. When you experiment, continue to try different things. Take mental or written notes on what works more often, and what doesn't work. When you figure out one problem, move on to the next experiment. It is fun, entertaining, and you will learn fast from it. Finding interesting experiments to perform in your daily life can be quite interesting and rewarding.

Principle #12: Value knowledge and practices that have stood the test of time.

Humans are constantly learning and teaching each other the new things that we learn. But we have to keep in mind our track record. At one time we thought the Earth was flat. At one time we didn't realize germs were spread through contact and that we should wash our hands. At another time many people believed the same creatures had always lived on the planet (rather than evolution). Of course, often newer findings may be accurate, but it can be a mistake to assume that all newer findings are accurate. In science, often one study appears to confirm something radical. A problem happens when further studies try to confirm those findings and fail — and we are forced to realize that the original experiment had an error. Also, keep in mind that the media often reports on new findings either with wrong facts and interpretations, or they may exaggerate the implications of a minor finding to try to gain readers. If you stay up to date with the latest findings, maintain your skepticism.

Principle #13: Practice questioning the things in life that we tend to take for granted as being normal and sensible.

Seek answers for yourself or from those around you. For example, consider your cultural traditions and practices, your religion, the layout of your towns, etc. When you question deeply, you sometimes find that there are many possible ways to approach any given topic or field. For example, some cultures have gotten along fine without technology even in modern times. There are so many ways a town or city could be built, that why do they all pretty much have the same setup? Sometimes when we question enough, we can find a better way to do things. Perhaps we can even think up an invention or a whole new way of doing things that most people missed.

Principle #14: We almost always have imperfect information on hand with which to make decisions.

Pretty much every real life decision that comes up can go an infinite amount of directions. You simply can't calculate or know for sure what will happen based on your actions. There are way too many variables. Just to name a few, there are reactions of anyone involved, unexpected setbacks (bad weather, a car accident), and your level of training may not have prepared you to make a good decision in the first place. How people deal with this inability to know what will happen is super important to their life success. We can start by looking at how to tackle the few examples I mentioned above. We need to learn how to read people better, and know if they can help us take the right actions. We need to avoid unexpected setbacks as much as possible, perhaps by driving extra carefully in bad weather. We also need to be aware of our own training and background, and gauge if we are prepared for any given challenge. If we are underprepared, we need to make it known or seek out help in making decisions.

Something important to realize is that instinctual or intuitive processes may carry more weight than trying to think logically through every problem that comes up. We often see intuitive people as less logical and less accurate in their approach, but the reality may be different. People who make quick intuitive decisions often realize that there is a lot of imperfect information they have to deal with. This means they don't have the complete information to know what to do. To have the complete information would literally mean to see the future and know what the outcome of any action would be. None of us can do this. Often times experts can make intuitive decisions well, but novices need more time to try to evaluate the scenario. We have to learn to deal with the fact that we can never know for sure what the results of our actions will be. Get used to making decisions with imperfect information on hand. It is a valuable skill to have.

Principle #15: Consider opposing perspectives to the ones you normally hold.

Try to mentally take the place of someone who holds another perspective, or who lives life in the opposing camp to your own. Just thinking more deeply about their daily lives and why they believe what they believe can be mind opening. Another important way to expand your horizons is to read up on how people in the opposing camp think about the issue. What kind of books, sites, and television stations do they get their information from? You can start there to get closer to understanding how they think. Make the effort to understand more deeply, rather than dismiss their beliefs and concerns offhand. Realize that you cannot truly disagree with someone's viewpoint until you completely understand what it is that they believe and why they believe it. Also realize that if you always get your information from the people who hold your own views, then you are missing out on getting a bigger picture understanding.

Principle #16: You have complete responsibility over yourself.

There will not always be someone else to guide you along. You need to learn to acquire and maintain your basic necessities, even if no one else is there to help. As children, we learn early on to rely on our guardians for help with everything. They shelter us, feed us, and watch after us in every way. As we get older we need to realize that we have full responsibility over ourselves. Fortunately, we do live in societies where everyone takes a small piece of the responsibility for all of us. This allows many of us to have peace of mind most of the time. We expect stores to carry food, the police to catch criminals, and generally for things to be orderly and predictable in society.

The reality is that anything can happen. The future is unforeseeable. Everyone is responsible for themselves first before others (the exception being if you have young children), and that means if a truly unpredicted situation happens, people will watch out for themselves first. Because of this, you would need to take care of your own needs too, since everyone else would be too busy taking care of themselves. A few situations that can happen are a need for you to defend yourself, a need to find your own food, or a need to survive in extreme weather. Our ancestors had instincts that we are losing because of our comfortable lives in modern society. It is dangerous to become too comfortable. Part of being truly intelligent is preparing for the unpredictable and unexpected.

Principle #17: Compare different systems to each other and ask yourself how they are similar or dissimilar.

You can consider systems such as the human body, the universe, the ecosystem, etc. This will broaden your understanding of more and more topics. Many systems can have unexpected similarities that can be easy to miss if you don't make the conscious effort to make connections. Take the human brain and computer programming, for example. Computer code is in binary, this means that 0's and 1's are used to encode whether a feature is on or off. The brain has a similar feature. Neurons guide our thought processes and brain functions, but they are designed either to fire or not fire (turn on or off). Therefore, neurons and computer code have a core similarity. The smallest components of both act fairly simply, but when compounded into networks of billions of 0s and 1s, or billions of neurons that fire and don't fire, the possibilities are endless. These kinds of connections can help you see how fields that seem completely different actually have some things in common. Making broad connections is often a key to making a creative breakthrough. In this case, knowledge of these different fields could be used to make new discoveries in the field of artificial intelligence.

Principle #18: Know the difference between mistakes and failure.

Many people have a fear of making mistakes and failing. But we should realize that they are not the same thing. Mistakes are errors we make, but they help us learn something new. Failure is giving up on ourselves, or being too scared to take a risk and give ourselves a real chance for success.

Often when we make mistakes, someone is there to tell us how foolish we were. Really, making mistakes is a natural and essential part of learning. Don't worry about people who tease you or discourage you when you make mistakes. They are ignorant to think that mistakes are a sign of failure or of doing something wrong. Often, people who make the most mistakes and who learn from them, are the ones that are the most successful and innovative in their field. The Wright Brothers for example, learned to make better and better planes through trial and error. They had countless crashes, but they learned from them, and they changed the world. Of course, you don't always need to make every mistake yourself. You can learn from seeing other people make mistakes too.

You should learn to see patterns in the kinds of mistakes you tend to make. Analyze the kinds of mistakes you are more prone to making, and ask yourself why they happen. Mistakes are learning tools. To fail is to give up on something prematurely. To fail is to avoid risks so much that you never make mistakes, and to never allow yourself to succeed in any important way.

Principle #19: Do not restrict your own potential.

If you expand your mind into believing that you can achieve something greater, then you can. The greatest minds never accept that they are only smart enough to reach a certain level of accomplishment. They push beyond any boundaries. They push themselves further and further until they make progress. Then they rest and do it again the next day. They learn every day, and they think about problems they believe are critical every day.

Einstein is well known to have thought about the speed of light and the nature of space-time every day. When his mind grappled with a problem, he didn't let it go until he understood it fully. Despite that he is one of the most well-known geniuses, he didn't learn to talk until he was four, and he failed many classes in his youth. Einstein would have had just as much reason as anyone else to believe that he wasn't cut out to be a genius. But he did not let anything stop him from what he wanted to achieve, and he will never be forgotten for his contribution to the world. Do not restrict yourself. Do not set limits on what you are capable of. You are capable of more than you know.

Principle #20: Use your talents and abilities for your own purpose.

Live for your own causes, and you will accomplish more than if you live for the cause of someone else. People in our lives that try to help us on the right path mean well, but we have to live our own lives. It is very easy to suggest to someone that they might like doing X, or they might like the money in Y, or that there is a lot of demand in Z right now. Trends come and go. One big money making field now could be nonexistent in 10 years or less. The people who know us best can sometimes offer useful guidance. However, you should keep in mind that you are the one who needs to put in the effort, show up to work, and deal with any challenges along the way, not whoever recommended a certain path.

Principle #21: Plenty of ideas are great in theory, but fail horribly in practice.

Ideas are fun to discuss, and to play around with in our minds, but to really know the value of an idea we have to test it somehow. Often times one test run isn't enough. An idea might appear to be good at first, and later turn out to be unsustainable. Some ideas require help from many sources, but the more people or agencies that get involved in making an idea run, the more chances there are for problems that put a stop to it. Communism is a good example of an idea that did not go as planned. It was thought that this system would sustain everyone and keep all of society satisfied in many countries. However, the reality was that the system was vulnerable to corruption, and it discouraged people from doing their best work because they wouldn't be rewarded for it.

Most ideas involve people in some way. For example, people will come up with the idea, execute the idea, and they will use the end product or the end system. The issue is that people at all stages tend to be unpredictable and they make mistakes. You can't know for sure what people want, and how they will react to something new, and you also can't account for unforeseen challenges along the way to making an idea happen. Be careful with your new ideas. Test them on a smaller scale before you invest heavily into them.

Principle #22: All the thoughts and planning in the world are of limited use.

There are too many variables for anyone to truly know the outcome of almost any event. Something that seems like it should fail often succeeds. And something that seems like it should work often does not. Planning and thinking ahead are good to do. They help us be prepared. Sometimes, however, people find comfort in thinking more and more, and analyzing possibilities more and more, and they get caught in a rut. Rather than progressing and stepping out into the real world and risk making mistakes, they stay in their comfort zone, and delay action.

We need to catch ourselves if we enter such a rut. We need to see it for what it is and push ourselves to try something, and to accept whatever outcome happens. Of course, if the stakes are super high and it is a matter of life and death, it is probably wise to have a complete plan from beginning to end to make sure no unforeseen problems arise. In other cases, remember that there is always a lot to learn from trying something and making a mistake, and then making corrections as we go.

Principle #23: If you often think abstractly, consider the concrete tangible reality. If you often think concretely, consider the world of ideas.

It may be most useful to bridge the two styles. Most of us actually have a tendency toward one or the other. It may have to do with our upbringing. If you grew up in a house of professors, you are probably used to thinking in concepts. If you grew up in a house of farmers, you may be more used to dealing with real world things, like animals and plants. Both ways are important to getting along in the world. Tangible things make up reality, and so we have to be familiar with them and know how they work. Abstract concepts and ideas help us understand broader areas more quickly, without needing to literally see them or touch them. When we use both ways of thinking, we acquire a more accurate view of the real world for what it is.

Principle #24: Be aware of your surroundings.

Although Sherlock Holmes is fictional, he is an interesting character to see in action. Many times he notices something present that does not fit with the expected context. Other times, he finds something absent that normally should be present in a given context. He observes very carefully, very analytically, and sees things most people would miss. You really never know what you can miss if you aren't looking around. Most of us get so caught up in our own lives that we fail to "smell the roses", as they say. Being more aware of your surroundings is good for your survival, and maybe even for finding unexpected gems. Perhaps you'll notice a new restaurant you missed, or see a baby smiling at you, or see an old friend you almost didn't notice. Life isn't always all work. Take a moment to look around and learn from what the world has to show you.

Principle #25: Exercise your brain by acting as if everything is important.

Everything you do and every experience you have is potentially important. Everything everyone says is potentially vital, and if you were more focused on thinking of a television show you wanted to watch later, you could miss it. By considering everything as important, you may learn more. People with photographic memories often describe a feeling that in their minds nothing is ever less or more important than something else. Because of this, they are able to remember everything exactly as it happened.

Usually, our brains naturally tell us that X information is important, and Y isn't. In this case, X might be a new work assignment, and Y might be choosing if you want to eat cereal or oatmeal for breakfast. Most of the time what your brain decides is probably correct. Some things are more important than others, naturally. But every once in a while you can be wrong, and something that you thought *was* important actually *was not*, or vice versa. Try acting as if everything is potentially important for one day, and see how it affects your thinking.

Principle #26: When you come across a word or term you do not know, look it up.

We live in an age where we have the privilege to look anything up in mere seconds. Many people have quick access to great resources in their own home. Some of the best resources are a dictionary, a thesaurus, and Wikipedia (or a general encyclopedia as a substitute). Of course, if you don't have these in your own home, you can find them at a library. Vocabulary is closely linked to intelligence, and there is a clear reason for this. The more words and terms you know, the easier it is to understand new concepts and ideas. Learn new words so you can expand your learning and your understanding.

Principle #27: We all harbor our own false ways of viewing the world.

We hold false beliefs about ourselves, other people, and the world. We are imperfect creatures and so this is inevitable. Never feel that you know everything, or that you are better than anyone else. For all we think that we know, we are probably only aware of a very small percentage of the true reality that is right in front of us. Think of the fact that all of the creatures in the world have a different perceptual system. Why do they perceive the world the way they do? Is it because their senses give them the truest view of the world? Not at all. Every creature out there only experiences the world through its own senses. It has no idea about any other way of perceiving.

If you follow the evolutionary theory, it makes sense that our evolution has driven us to a perceptual system that allows us to survive in our environment. This applies to all animals. For example, think about how we perceive objects as 3-D shapes, but we only actually see the surfaces of them. We can smell, but only within the close range around us. We only feel that which comes into contact with us personally. The range of information we have is very limited, and very prone to inaccuracies.

Remember that we do not experience everything accurately, as it actually is. We only need to look up 'logical fallacies' or 'cognitive biases' on Wikipedia to recognize just how many common misperceptions we have. The best we can do is realize this fact, and never allow ourselves to feel that we know it all.

Principle #28: The brain needs challenges to grow.

It is like a muscle in that way. The brain has plasticity, meaning it is very adaptable to different needs depending on how you use it. If you think about all of the different kinds of animals that exist, many of them specialize in something. They tend to be specialists in finding or catching a few different kinds of food. Humans are generalists. We can train ourselves to do so many things that to try to make a list of the possibilities would be quite difficult. The more challenges you face, the more chances you will have to excel in different areas. Playing Chess, or figuring out math problems can certainly exercise your brain, but so can juggling. There are many ways to challenge your brain. Don't assume that one way is necessarily better than another.

Generally, if you find something that engages you and challenges you, it is helping your brain. It could be either a physical or mental activity. If you learn something passively, or do an activity without much thought, it will not provide the proper challenge. Challenge your brain and your mind will expand.

Principle #29: Life is exciting, fascinating, and magical.

If you take a path that steers you away from seeing this, you might want to reconsider what you are doing. There will never be anyone else quite like you. No one else will ever see the world quite like you, or do exactly what you do. Realize that some of the greatest geniuses had abundant energy within themselves. They needed to have this energy in order to work as much as they did and to reach the levels of understanding and achievement that they did. The world around us, and the life that is right in front of us can act as an inspiration for us to truly make a difference.

Some geniuses love life so much that they see it as their mission to protect it, and so they work as biologists or political activists. Other geniuses such as Leonardo da Vinci were so inspired by life that they created some of the greatest art works of all time. Use life to inspire you, to make connections, to understand, and to relate to everything in a deeper way. And don't forget that you too are a part of this experience we call life.

Principle #30: Focus on gaining a depth of knowledge rather than just acquiring superficial tidbits.

The culture today is constantly bombarded by flashy and quick bits of knowledge. One day one thing is the big craze to know, the next day it is something else - these are mostly useless to have. They are interesting factoids that might help start a conversation, but they are not the way to build true knowledge and understanding. Einstein was once asked how many feet are in a mile. He said "I don't know, why should I fill my brain with facts I can find in two minutes in any standard reference book?" He had a point. Knowing *random* details about an assortment of topics has a limited use.

Today you don't even need a reference book, Google will have the answers as fast as you can type your question. The point is we should pick what we really want to learn, and immerse ourselves in that topic. Learn as much as you can, to the point that you've truly gained something worth knowing, something that you can apply in your daily life.

Principle #31: Think about how you personally affect the world around you.

Simply by existing we consume other life forms every day. We alter our environments by taking up space and using trees for our homes and paper. People that are more conscious need to find a higher purpose after realizing how much we can consume without even noticing it. Living a life of self-gratification isn't as satisfying when you realize that everything you do affects the rest of the world. Many of us use gasoline, a nonrenewable resource. Many of us use a vehicle that releases carbon and that plays a role in global warming. Many of us also throw out trash that ends up in huge landfills or in the ocean. We can choose to help the world, or ignore the issues, but either way we all have an effect. It takes someone who is self-aware, and aware of the world to realize that even though he or she is just one person out of billions, that it is possible to have a positive impact. It is possible to make a difference for the better, for ourselves, our children, and our future. We simply need to educate ourselves further, take action, and encourage others to do the same.

Principle #32: Record your thoughts and observations.

Leonardo da Vinci had a massive collection of notes on his observations, sketches for inventions, and his own thoughts. He wrote something down almost every day, accumulating many journals of material in his life. If you are curious to see some of his recordings, there is a compilation called *Leonardo's Notebooks*. Thomas Edison is another genius who took prolific notes. He took very detailed notes on his ideas about electricity, light bulbs, and anything else he thought could be important. All in all, there are five million pages of his notes held as part of the United States historical record. These were two great and prolific geniuses, and they consistently documented what they learned.

Realize that notes and writing provide a record not only for yourself, but if you were to make a great breakthrough (or even if not), others could use them as well. It is recommended to have a notebook, a blog, or even an audio recorder to document anything that seems to be important. Something interesting about writing down ideas and thoughts is that the more you record, the more new ideas and thoughts pop into your mind. One of them might even be the breakthrough idea of a genius.

Principle #33: Learn to practice effectively for more efficient learning.

To really learn a skill we have to practice it. To learn even faster and more effectively, we have to know what to focus on when we practice. It helps to have an expert around who can guide us and give feedback. Usually, what they will do is tell us the most crucial parts of the task that need to be met before anything else can be accomplished. For example, in typing it is critical to have your hands in the right position so you hit the keys you are supposed to. In piano, you should be aware of the hand positioning for a song as well as maintaining a relaxed posture — being relaxed helps to move the fingers more fluidly and to avoid injuries.

Often times when we practice something over and over, we see patterns and find that we have weaknesses. Many people will avoid their weak areas because it is a challenge. They will instead practice what they are good at, so they feel better. As you might guess, it is actually a better use of our time to focus on improving our weak areas when we practice a new skill. In doing this, you can advance more quickly. To practice effectively we should identify the most essential parts of the task, begin practice, identify our weaknesses, practice some more, and continue to seek feedback from experts. As you get better you may create something new. In that case, you can get feedback from an audience as well. Do not forget that the quality of your practice is much more important than the quantity. With focus, you will not need to practice as much to reach mastery.

Principle #34: Don't overwhelm your natural ability to learn.

If you cram too much information in your head all at once you will not learn well. If you stress yourself too much you also may not be at your best. True learning that is valuable and useful for a lifetime builds up gradually, not all at once. You need to have time to connect what you learn to other things. Cramming, or spending long nonstop sessions working or learning something is not optimal. Taking breaks is not lazy. Our minds need some time to breathe and relax.

Remember, the brain is like a muscle. Weight trainers that exercise their muscles every day train different muscles and they take breaks after training. They do not consistently exhaust the same muscle over and over. The brain should be treated similarly, rather than completely straining it. For example, Einstein was a notoriously hard worker, focusing intensely for great periods. But even he had a point where he needed a break to do something completely different. For him, that was often playing his violin.

Principle #35: When you get a great idea, ask yourself if the timing is right to execute it.

Will the public be ready for your idea? Imagine that you are living around the time of 1800 in Europe, a time when classical music was popular. If classical music was all you had ever heard, would you be interested in jazz, or techno, or hip hop? It would probably seem too wild and crazy, and maybe even hurt your ears. We learn to adapt to what is new, often through a gradual process, not in giant leaps. If an idea is too advanced, too far ahead of its time, the public often won't understand the use, or they may not believe that it's really possible.

Even if someone came out with an invention to teleport us tomorrow, would you really be willing to try it out so quickly? Maybe it would make sense if we progressed through decades from teleporting nanoparticles, to molecules, to flies, to rodents. But to just all of a sudden have a mechanism for teleporting people safely seems unbelievable. When you get a great idea, ask yourself if the public is ready. Is this an idea they can relate to and understand? Or is there a way you can convince them that your idea solves a problem they have.

Principle #36: Know your strengths and weaknesses, and how to make them work for you.

Everyone has strengths and weaknesses. Some common areas of strength and weakness are self-confidence, social skills, management skills, and a variety of technical skills. Depending on what you want to do, you might not need to fix your weaknesses. If you are a manager, sometimes it is okay not to fully understand all of the technicalities. It is more important to be able to get a team to accomplish the necessary work. Of course, if the weakness is a critical area that you need to perform your daily tasks, then it is important to work on improving it.

Your strengths are also important to recognize. If you are naturally good at speaking, but not at writing, you can steer yourself toward positions that play up your natural presentational abilities. Be aware of your general strengths and weaknesses, and how you compare to your peers. Also pay attention to which strengths and weaknesses are most critical for what you want to accomplish. Focusing on the critical skill sets will help you reach your goals more easily.

Principle #37: Pay attention to overall patterns, and the anomalies that do not fit.

Life largely consists of patterns and anomalies. The patterns are the general structures, the things you expect to see because you've seen them happen so many times before. In fact, our brains often naturally pick up general patterns and tendencies. Once you know what to expect quite well, you will be prepared to notice anomalies, the things or events that don't fit with the context. Often, by realizing that there is an anomaly present, we can further investigate it. Darwin realized on his voyage studying other life forms that there were many minor variations among different species of birds. This was inconsistent with his prior worldview that we were all fixed species that never changed form. He took that anomaly and investigated it further, founding the theory of evolution.

Geniuses learn the patterns, the tendencies of a system, and if they come across an anomaly they do not discard it. They focus on it until they understand why it happened. Often times it is the unexpected anomaly that leads to a great breakthrough of a discovery.

Principle #38: Persist through the desire to give up on your ambitions.

Geniuses make the choice to persist through obstacles, taking themselves further and further into the unknown. They take themselves gleefully into places where they are not even sure how they will ever get out safely. They may work on a problem that they feel is completely beyond them, and dedicate years or decades of their lives to it. Einstein spent a great deal of time contemplating issues of the universe, for example. He took the risk of investing so much of his time with the possibility that in the end he would have nothing to show for it. He pushed through any pain or fear, and continued.

Many great geniuses reach a point where they feel alone and that it would be better just to give up. The reality is that the greatest problems are not easy to solve. They take great persistence. The great geniuses ultimately realize this, and so they don't give up. They push themselves completely, and they take their minds beyond where most of ours will ever go. To take your mind to the greatest enlightenment and reach the greatest revelations, it takes real mental effort over time.

You can practice this skill by starting small. When you find a stubborn homework problem, or you have a problem fixing a broken system of any kind, don't stop at the first obstacle. Persist until you figure it out. Learn to persist through pain, boredom, fear, and strain, to keep going and going. Press on until you reach a solution. Then take that mental training and tough skin with you to whatever great problem you set your mind to.

Principle #39: When you give up on a problem and quit looking for solutions is often when you will find the answer.

Sometimes geniuses become so focused on a problem that they will not rest until they find the solution. They may stay up nights, seclude themselves, and fixate on an issue, cycling it in their minds over and over. Some geniuses are so persistent that they do not know when to give it a rest. They will continue above and beyond what any normal person would tolerate. Many times, they take their field personally. They believe solving a specific problem is important beyond just for their own reasons, and this motivates them to continue despite a lack of progress. What tends to surprise many great minds is that at the moment they completely give up on a problem, and their mind relaxes, they often see the answer in a flash.

Chess players often talk about how right after they make their move, they immediately see a better move that they should have made. This is because they stopped looking for solutions, and all of a sudden the right way popped into the mind when they just relaxed their thoughts. As strange as it sounds, sometimes relaxing your mind and your thoughts is the best thing you can do to find your solution.

Principle #40: Spread knowledge, the importance of it, and a love for it.

When you learn something that changes your life for the better, or that blows you away with how much it expands your understanding, share it. Many people in today's society don't read, and aren't curious about very much outside the things that immediately impact them. If you can get someone else interested in learning or knowledge, you've made a big difference in this world.

Anytime you find someone who wants to learn something you know, offer to teach them. It helps them, of course, but we also learn a great deal by teaching others. We make better connections and we stretch ourselves by answering the tough questions that curious minds ask. You should tell people, especially young people, how important it is to always be learning. Tell them how knowledge and learning impacted your life. One way to share your love of knowledge is to share or give away a book that had a big impact on you.

Final Thoughts

These are the principles that the great geniuses have laid out for us to follow. I have merely noticed them, collected them, and explained them for your benefit. Of course, not all circumstances are alike. A principle that works well in one case may not work quite as well in another. You would be wise to evaluate which principles would be most helpful to your life right now. It would be a worthy investment to choose several principles that you can begin testing out for yourself. The best principles will be the ones that you can apply and benefit from. They will be the ones that enlighten you to a better path, and bring you greater rewards. The principles themselves are of course useless unless you apply them.

True geniuses are always pushing boundaries and testing the waters. They are curious and experimental, always learning something new. If you proceed on that kind of journey toward genius, you will likely encounter your own new tools to add to the toolkit that has been presented here. I would encourage you as you find new tools on your own, to leave them behind in comments or reviews of this book for other readers to benefit from. Or if you are feeling more ambitious, keep a log over time and write your own book.

I. C. Robledo

With the intellectual tools you've learned, you are now prepared to embark on your own path toward genius. Just remember that being a genius is not so much a goal in itself. What I've learned from studying geniuses is that they pick an issue that is of great importance to them, and they tackle it with all of their will and persistence. True geniuses are not so concerned with whether they are seen as a genius or not. This mindset frees them to take calculated risks and increase their chances of making a major breakthrough.

Thank You

Thank you for taking the time to read *The Intellectual Toolkit of Geniuses*. I hope that you found the information useful. Just remember that a key part of the learning process is putting what you read into practice.

Before you go, I want to invite you to pick up your free copy of *Step Up Your Learning: Free Tools to Learn Almost Anything*. All you have to do is type this link into your browser:

http://bit.ly/Robledo

Also, if you have any questions, comments, or feedback about this book, you can send me a message and I'll get back to you as soon as possible. Please put the title of the book you are commenting on in the subject line. My email address is:

ic.robledo@mentalmax.net

Did You Learn Something New?

If you found value in this book, please review it on Amazon so I can stay focused on writing more great books. Even a short one or two sentences would be helpful.

To go directly to the review page, you may type this into your web browser:

http://hyperurl.co/4b0ryt

An Invitation to the "Master Your Mind" Community (on Facebook)

I founded a community where we can share advice or tips on our journey to mastering the mind. Whether you want to be a better learner, improve your creativity, get focused, or work on other such goals, this will be a place to find helpful information and a supportive network. I hope you join us and commit to taking your mind to a higher level.

To go directly to the page to join the community, you may type this into your web browser:

http://hyperurl.co/xvbpfc

More Books by I. C. Robledo

Smart Life Book Bundle (Books 1-6) – includes the following:

The Intellectual Toolkit of Geniuses

Master Your Focus

The Smart Habit Guide

No One Ever Taught Me How to Learn

55 Smart Apps to Level Up Your Brain

Ready, Set, Change

The Secret Principles of Genius

Idea Hacks

Practical Memory

To see the full list of authored books, visit:

www.Amazon.com/author/icrobledo

Made in the USA
Las Vegas, NV
06 February 2021